MW00596440

Little
Hawaiian
Hurry Up & Wait
Cookbook

Betty Shimabukuro & Joleen Oshiro

MUTUAL PUBLISHING

This book is an abridgement of
Hurry Up and Wait (published in 2013)

ISBN: 978-1939487-34-6

Library of Congress Control Number:
2014938661

Photos from Dreamstime.com:
   pg. 13 © Klenova, pg. 25
   © Elena Elisseeva, pg.
   31 © Jianghongyan, pg.
   57 © Zkruger, pg. 63 ©
   Msphotographic, pg. 83 ©
   Robyn Mackenzie

First Printing, October 2014

Mutual Publishing, LLC
1215 Center Street, Suite 210
Honolulu, Hawai'i 96816
Ph: 808-732-1709
Fax: 808-734-4094
info@mutualpublishing.com
www.mutualpublishing.com

Printed in South Korea

Table of Contents

Desserts & Snacks

Wiki Cooking

Joleen Oshiro

t was a couple of years ago that I was introduced to the wonders of the pressure cooker while writing a food story for the *Honolulu Star-Advertiser*. Here was a device, I was told, that could deliver stew in 20 minutes or a roast in an hour. Be still my beating heart! Like so many working folks, commuting to and from town for work, and in my case, driving a child to school across the island, my family ate way too many fast-food meals. It was a strain on our pocketbook, not to mention our health, and I felt awful that our dinners were at odds with locavore values.

So, not long after that story published, I purchased my first pressure cooker, a six-quart Fagor brand pot for which I got a double discount and a rebate—a $100 cooker for $30. As do most brands, Fagor says its cookers decrease cooking time by at least 30 percent, and I've found this to be true.

Here are some things to know about pressure cookers.

How a pressure cooker works:

- The pressure cooker offers a faster cooking process, between 30 and 70 percent less cooking time. When its lid is sealed and locked, steam produced by heating liquid builds pressure, and that pressure raises the boiling temperature from 212 to 250°F. The increase in temperature breaks down food fibers about one-third faster than standard cooking. And because of the sealed environment, more nutrients and flavors stay within the food rather than escaping with the steam.

- This manner of cooking saves energy as well. Here's why: After a pot hits high pressure, heat must be lowered to regulate pressure, lest the dish burn and the cooker suffer damage. Lower heat plus shorter cooking time equals less energy use.

Types of pressure cookers:

- My pot has a spring-valve pressure regulator, which involves a colored cylinder that pops up to indicate when pressure is reached. Another type is the "jiggle-top" in which a metal weight sits on the cooker's vent pipe. When the pot hits pressure, the weight jiggles. A third resembles a jiggle-top, but the regulator doesn't jiggle, requiring that the pot be carefully monitored to determine when it reaches pressure.

- All types have safety latches that cannot be unlocked until pressure is released. This prevents the explosions of food that occurred with pressure cookers of the past.

Important features:

- Find a cooker that operates at fourteen to sixteen pounds per square inch (psi) when it hits high pressure, since the standard pressure used in recipes is fifteen psi. Lower psi can substantially extend cooking time. Good-quality pots are constructed of 18/10 stainless steel and have three-ply bottoms that include a layer of aluminum or copper to promote even heating, which is important to prevent scorching.

Cooking tips:

- Because steam is vital to the cooking process, most pressure cookers require one-half to one cup of liquid in the pot when in use. While selecting a pot, look for one that won't require much more liquid, or dishes could end up watery.

- Fill pots no more than two-thirds full. There needs to be space in the cavity for pressure to build.

- The pressure cooker is an ideal way to cook beans. Not only does it dramatically decrease cooking time, it delivers beans that are well cooked without loss of flavor. When preparing beans, fill the pot no more than halfway, and add a tablespoon or two of oil to control the foam that is produced during the cooking process. Many online pressure-cooking sites and cookbooks recommend presoaking beans, but I never do. I just follow my resource for cooking times: a chart composed by author Lorna Sass, in my personal pressure-cooking bible, *Pressure Perfect*. (She includes charts for meats, vegetables and grains as well in her cookbooks.) Most pressure cookers come with manuals or cookbooks that include general cooking times.

- There are several ways to release pressure, depending on how much residual cooking time a dish requires, because food continues to cook in a pressurized environment with high temperature even when the pot is removed from the heat source.

- One way to finish off the cooking process is to allow the pot to come to a "natural-pressure release," meaning the lid remains sealed until the pot cools enough for pressure to diffuse. This method is used regularly for cooking proteins and beans.

- Quick-pressure release involves opening a valve on the cooker. But the fastest way to release pressure is to run water from a faucet over the lid of the pot. Within seconds, pressure is diffused. This method allows for proper cooking of vegetables that would otherwise end up overcooked.

Accessories and tools:

- Use inserts to expand the possibilities of pressure cooking. Trivets, which raise a pan or bowl off the bottom of the pot, allow for cooking casserole-type dishes or foods that would overcook or burn if heated directly in the pot. Some foods are best cooked in foil packets on a trivet or in a steamer basket. These include fish fillets, or potatoes to be added to longer-cooking stews or curries.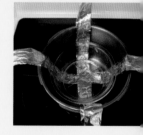

- When cooking something in a bowl or pan, use foil strips to retrieve the dish from the heated pot. This tip comes from Sass: Cut two long pieces aluminum foil. Fold them crosswise to make long strips. Lay the strips over the trivet across each other to form an "x," so four strips are coming out of the pot. Place the dish on top of the strips. Tuck the ends into the pot, cover and seal. When food is done, straighten out the four foil strips and grab them to lift out the dish.

Slo 'Ono
Betty Shimabukuro

For decades I tried to develop a meaningful relationship with my slow cooker, but it was an inconsistent partner. A great meal here, a mediocre one there. Rapture and rejection for so many years.

Sometime in 2010 I decided, enough of that. I looked my Crock-Pot square in the eye (which is somewhere around the temperature knob) and said, "Prove yourself to me, or I am turning your space over to a food processor."

The pot having no free will or opposable thumbs, however, meant the proving was left to me. I spent months combing cookbooks and searching online sources, and I tried to use the dang thing once a week.

In 2011 I launched a Crock-Pot crusade in the *Honolulu Star-Advertiser* that became known as "Slow 'Ono." My goal: great, uncomplicated local-style slow-cooker meals. Readers were invited to submit recipes and requests, and I reported my top finds once a month. Those recipes became the start of this cookbook.

Why bother? Because a slow cooker can save money and energy. It allows you to cook a meal while absent from the house, which saves time even as it takes time. Nothing boils over and nothing burns (unless you are very neglectful). And low-heat, long cooking is supposed to be the best way to draw the most out of many foods.

Why is it so difficult? We expect too much from this partner. We want to toss some ingredients in the crock, turn it on, go to work, come home, and scoop out dinner, preferably delicious. We seek the holy grail—a dish that is at its prime after ten hours of cooking, equal to an eight-hour workday, plus commute. We want it to be effortless.

It is this singular pursuit that leaves so many people dissatisfied with their slow cookers. Truth is, most dishes peak after six to eight hours of cooking (less for chicken), with overcooking leading to blah results. And sometimes a dish is improved by attention midway through, such as turning the meat or adding ingredients, especially vegetables, that have shorter cooking times.

As for effortless? Often you'll be much happier with the finished product if you do a little bit of tweaking afterward (skim the fat, thicken the sauce, sometimes even broil the meat to give it some crusty chew).

Treat your slow cooker as a tool, not a solo workhorse, one that sometimes needs the assist of the range or microwave, and some understanding from you.

The two of you will be much happier together.

Choosing a slow cooker:

The two most common brands are Crock-Pot and Hamilton Beach. Both companies offer many models—from $20 to $200, with all kinds of features. All basically cook at two temperature settings, low and high, with a warm setting for finished dishes. They are simple machines, although some have timers, temperature sensors, even browning elements.

The recipes in this book were tested in basic models of

both brands. If you are buying your first, I would suggest a six- or seven-quart oval cooker, which is of a size and shape that can accommodate a large roast. If you need something smaller for a particular recipe you can place a casserole dish inside the crock. Be sure the slow cooker has a light that indicates the power is on (you'd be surprised how many lack this basic function). Other than that, you can get along without any other bells or whistles.

If you find you have an affinity for slow cooking you can investigate a fancier model.

{ Kickoff Cookoff }

A number of dishes considered standard fare in any local recipe lineup are well-suited for both the slow cooker and the pressure cooker. Four—Chicken Adobo, Chicken Long Rice, Shoyu Chicken, and Portuguese Bean Soup—are profiled here with recipes tailored for both appliances. While each recipe is distinctive, all exemplify the flavors that make these dishes all-time favorites.

If you have a slow cooker but no pressure cooker, or vice versa, compare these recipes. You may be persuaded to invite the other appliance into your home.

Chicken Adobo

Serves 6 to 8

While researching this dish, I couldn't believe its simplicity, reiterated in recipe after recipe. It's basically a combination of a few common ingredients in which the chicken is marinated, then cooked. While marinating takes several hours, cooking in the pressure cooker is only about 10 minutes. If you like, when the cooking is complete, turn up the heat and reduce the sauce. Adobo has a strong, bright flavor out of the pot, then settles into a lovely mellowness the next day.

4 to 5 pounds chicken thighs
1/2 cup white vinegar
1/2 cup soy sauce
1 tablespoon garlic powder
1 teaspoon peppercorns
3 bay leaves
1 tablespoon brown sugar

In bowl, combine ingredients well, then cover and marinate in refrigerator at least 1 hour, preferably 3 hours.

Transfer ingredients to pot. Cover, seal lid, and bring to pressure. Reduce heat and cook 8 to 10 minutes.

Remove from heat, allow natural-pressure release for 4 minutes, then quick-release pressure. Chicken should fall off the bone easily.

Chicken Adobo

Serves 6

The usual local version of adobo is chicken or pork simmered in a simple vinegar-based sauce. Traditional Filipino recipes will sometimes include coconut milk or sugar—and they often call for broiling, grilling or frying the meat at the end to crisp the outside.

This recipe calls for marinating as a first step, and in the end broiling the chicken and thickening the sauce. All this is meant to intensify the flavor, but if it's too fussy for you, just throw all the ingredients in the crock and cook. Eat it straight out of the pot. You'll still be satisfied.

4 pounds chicken thighs, skin removed, bone-in (see note)
1 large onion, sliced
1 teaspoon pepper
3 tablespoons tapioca starch or cornstarch dissolved in
   3 tablespoons water

Marinade:
1-1/2 cups cider vinegar
1/2 cup soy sauce
3 cloves garlic, minced

Combine marinade ingredients. Pour over chicken pieces and let marinate, refrigerated, at least 4 hours.

Place onions in bottom of slow cooker. Top with chicken and sprinkle with pepper. Pour marinade over all. Cook on low 4 to 5 hours, until chicken is tender. Turn pieces halfway through, if possible.

(If cooking ahead to serve on another day, refrigerate chicken and onions separately from juices. When ready to serve, remove fat from sauce and proceed with the next steps.)

Place chicken on broiling pan and broil 5 minutes per side until lightly browned.

Meanwhile, skim fat from liquid in slow cooker. Place liquid in small pot on stove; bring to simmer. Dissolve tapioca or cornstarch in water and stir into pot, continuing to stir until mixture thickens. Serve chicken with onions and pour sauce over all.

{ FOR PORK ADOBO } The same marinade can be used with pieces of pork cut in cubes. Cooking time will be 4 to 6 hours.

{ NOTE } Removing the skin from chicken pieces helps cut the fat in the dish, but if left on the skin crisps up under the broiler. Your choice.

Portuguese Bean Soup

Serves 8

The inspiration for this recipe came from a friendly stranger I chatted with in the supermarket. While I was perusing kabocha, she shared that one of the best things she makes with the pumpkin is Portuguese bean soup. Though at first thought that might seem odd, kabocha contributes a mellow sweetness that adds a subtle depth of flavor. Just a small amount, diced very small so that it melts into the broth, makes a world of difference, she insisted. Then she pointed at the kale and said there wasn't any better green to add to the pot. I've tested this recipe on various friends and relatives, and they agree.

2 cups dried navy beans
15 cups water, divided
2 tablespoons oil, divided
1 large onion, diced
1 cup celery, diced
2 medium carrots, diced
1 (10-ounce) Portuguese sausage, peeled of casing and cubed
3 to 4 hamhocks
1/2 cup kabocha, small dice
1 (14.5-ounce) can diced tomatoes
1 (8-ounce) can tomato sauce
2 medium potatoes, large dice
Salt and pepper, to taste
1 bunch kale, sliced into strips

Cook beans: Place beans into pressure-cooker pot. Add 6 cups water and 1 tablespoon oil. Seal lid, bring to pressure, lower heat, and cook 20 minutes. Remove from heat and allow natural-pressure release, about 20 minutes. Drain beans in colander and set aside.

On medium-high, heat rest of oil in pressure-cooker pot and add onions, celery and carrots. Sauté until onions soften. Remove to bowl and set aside.

Return pot to stove on medium-high heat and cook sausage. Remove to plate lined with paper towel and set aside.

Return pot to stove on high and add hamhocks, kabocha, and remaining 9 cups water. Seal lid, bring to pressure, lower heat, and cook 45 minutes. Remove from heat and allow natural-pressure release. Meat should be tender enough to fall off the bone. If not, reseal lid, return to heat, and cook another 10 minutes. Continue to check on hocks and cook until meat is extremely tender. Remove hocks from pot, shred or slice meat, discard bones, and return meat to pot.

Add diced tomatoes, tomato sauce, potatoes, and salt and pepper. Seal lid, bring to pressure, lower heat, and cook 1 minute. Quick-release pressure. Add kale, onion, carrots, and celery, reseal lid, bring to pressure, and quick-release pressure.

Open lid, and return navy beans and sausage to the pot. Simmer several minutes to reheat. Taste and adjust seasoning if necessary.

Portuguese Bean Soup

Serves 10

A couple of inexpensive ham hocks are the great beginnings of the best bean soup you will ever make. You start in the morning making a fabulous pork broth, then continue using that broth as the basis of your soup.

If you have a ham at Thanksgiving, this is a great Black Friday soup. Start the stock, using the ham bone, before going to bed. In the morning make the soup and let it cook all day while everyone's out and about. They all can feed themselves when they get home.

2 (15-ounce) cans kidney beans, with liquid
2 cups diced tomatoes (fresh or canned)
1 large onion, halved and cut in wedges
1 large potato, peeled and diced in 1/2-inch pieces (about 2 cups)
2 large carrots, peeled and sliced 1/2-inch thick (about 2 cups)
1 (15-ounce) can tomato sauce
12 ounces Portuguese sausage, in 1-inch slices
6 cups shredded kale

Stock:
2 ham hocks (or a leftover ham bone)
1 sprig rosemary
1 cup coarsely chopped cilantro (leaves and stems)
3 cloves garlic, peeled and crushed
2 cups water (see note)

Combine stock ingredients in 6-quart slow cooker. Cook on low at least 4 hours (longer cooking is OK, so you can let it simmer over-night).

Remove rose-mary stem from pot (most of the leaves will have fallen off). Remove ham hocks; debone, and chop meat, discarding large pieces of fat. Refrigerate meat.

Skim fat from liquid in pot. Add beans to pot along with all of the remaining ingredients except sausage and kale. Continue cooking on low 8 hours, or until vegetables are tender. Soup will hold on warm for several hours. Stir in cooked meat, sausage, and kale and cook another 30 minutes or until meat is heated through and kale is tender.

{ NOTE } If you think you will have a use for extra stock, use 4 to 6 cups water. After the stock is cooked and the fat skimmed, measure out 2 cups for the soup. Save the rest for another use. It makes a great base for stew or another soup.

{ TO SIMPLIFY } If you don't have all day for this, or if you can't be home after 4 hours to tend the pot, just put every-thing in at once (except the kale) and let it go for 8 to 10 hours. The stock won't be as flavorful, but what you don't know you can't miss.

Shoyu Chicken

Serves 8

Few dishes are more popular with the local crowd than Shoyu Chicken, an ultimate Hawai'i-style comfort food. Thanks to the pressure cooker, this staple can be on the weekday dinner table, flavorful and fork tender, in 30 minutes from beginning to end.

1 tablespoon olive oil
5 pounds chicken thighs, skin and fat removed
1 large onion, large dice
1-1/4 cups soy sauce
1/4 cup water
1 cup brown sugar
1-1/2 tablespoons garlic powder
1/2 to 1 teaspoon rock salt
1 finger ginger, peeled and smashed
2 tablespoons cornstarch, mixed with 2 tablespoons water

Place oil in pot and heat on high. Add chicken and onions and brown.

Meanwhile, in bowl, combine soy sauce, water, sugar, garlic powder, salt and ginger. Pour over chicken. Seal lid and on high heat bring pot to pressure. Lower heat and cook 15 minutes.

Remove pot from heat. Allow natural-pressure release for 4 minutes, then quick-release pressure. Open lid and test a piece of chicken with a fork; meat should easily flake with gentle pressure. If chicken isn't tender, pressure cook another 2 minutes.

Skim fat off top of sauce, or refrigerate chicken overnight and remove solidified fat.

When ready to eat, heat chicken and sauce. Remove chicken to serving bowl. Bring sauce to boil and add cornstarch mixture. Simmer, stirring until sauce is thickened, 2 to 3 minutes. Pour over chicken.

Shoyu Chicken

Serves 6

The trick to really good Shoyu Chicken was taught to me by Paul Masuoka, owner of the now defunct Masu's Massive Plate Lunch. He said to brown the chicken really well on really high heat—we're talking near-charred here. If your smoke detector goes off, you know you're doing it right, he told me. I do this on a portable gas burner outside—I'm not sure I know how to turn off my smoke detector.

4 to 5 pounds chicken thighs, skin removed, bone-in
1/4 cup water

Marinade:
1/2 cup soy sauce
1/4 cup mirin (sweet Japanese cooking wine)
1/4 cup brown sugar
3 cloves garlic, crushed and minced
1-inch piece ginger, crushed and minced
1/2 cup chopped cilantro, leaves and stems

Combine marinade ingredients. Pour over chicken. Marinate 4 hours in refrigerator.

Place large skillet over high heat. Remove chicken from marinade (reserving all the marinade). Brown chicken well. Remove chicken to to 6- or 7-quart slow cooker.

Add water to skillet and deglaze (scrape up the browned bits at bottom of pan). Pour contents of skillet over chicken along with all the reserved marinade. Cook on low 4 to 5 hours or until cooked through. Turn pieces halfway through.

To thicken sauce (optional): Remove chicken pieces and skim fat from liquid in crock. Thicken sauce on stove top using a slurry of 3 tablespoons cornstarch or tapioca starch dissolved in 1/4 cup water.

Chicken Long Rice

Serves 6

At my house, we don't need a spread of laulau, kālua pig, and lomi salmon to enjoy Chicken Long Rice. We eat it by itself and treat it like soup. In fact, it's one of my daughter's favorite comfort foods. Add plenty of ginger, and it's a great dish for someone under the weather. Though this recipe offers an option for incorporating chicken broth, it doesn't take much ambition or effort to make the broth from scratch, just 30 minutes of pressure cooking chicken wings, back, neck, or bones. For a broth with a touch of sweetness, add some carrots. While all this is happening, soak the long rice in boiling water, then simply add it in at the end and simmer 5 minutes. That way, you'll preserve the soupy quality of the dish.

2 (2-ounce) bundles long rice
3 quarts water (or substitute 3 to 4 cans chicken broth, or a combo of water and canned broth)
2-1/2 pounds bone-in chicken pieces
1 large onion, diced
3 tablespoons salt, or to taste (reduce salt if using canned broth)
3 to 4 shiitake mushrooms, soaked in water until soft, and sliced, stems removed; reserve water
2 tablespoons soy sauce
1 finger-size piece ginger, peeled and smashed, or to taste
1 tablespoon garlic powder, or to taste
Bamboo shoots (optional)
3 stalks green onion, chopped, for garnish

In large bowl, soak long rice bundles in boiling water. Set aside.

To pressure cooker pot, add water, chicken, onion, salt, shiitake and its reserved water, and soy sauce. Seal lid, bring to pressure, lower heat, and cook 10 minutes.

Quick-release pressure and remove chicken. Shred or remove meat from bone and slice into bite-sized pieces. Set aside.

Return bones to pot, add ginger and garlic powder; seal lid. Bring to pressure, lower heat, and cook 30 minutes.

Quick-release pressure, strain out bones, and return broth and pot to burner. Taste broth and adjust seasoning. Return chicken to pot.

Drain long rice and add to pot along with bamboo shoots if using. Cover with lid but do not seal. Simmer 5 minutes. Serve with topping of green onion.

Chicken Long Rice

Serves 8

This is a dish I usually skip at the lū'au table. I've always found it a bit blah compared with the bold flavors offered by other dishes. But this version, built on a broth made with a few chicken thighs and just a bit of ginger, is much tastier than the average. It is clear evidence of how a little extra effort yields much better slow-cooker results.

6 chicken thighs, bone-in, skin and excess fat removed

2-inch piece ginger, peeled, sliced, smashed

2 cups water

4 ounces long rice or bean thread noodles (2 small packages), soaked in water to soften

4 cups watercress (leaves and thin stems only; discard thick stems)

Place chicken and ginger in 5- or 6-quart slow cooker, add water. Cook on low 4 hours or until chicken is very tender (do not overcook or texture will suffer). Remove chicken, debone, and shred.

Add long rice and watercress to crock. Turn off and let sit 15 minutes. Noodles will absorb most of the liquid and watercress will wilt. Stir in shredded chicken.

{ The Soup Pot }

Soups lend themselves to pressure cooking because the cooker cuts down the time traditionally spent on everything from cooking beans to making stock. It takes just 30 to 60 minutes of pressure cooking bones to create delicious homemade stock. (Smaller bones, such as those from chicken, take less time than thick beef bones.) Add some aromatic vegetables if you want to round out the flavor.

Soups are an easy first dish for the slow cooker novice. They're simple: Let a few ingredients swim around in a lot of liquid for a long time. The same principle applies whether you're using a pot on the stove or your slow cooker. Just keep in mind that with slow cooking, liquids don't reduce, so flavors don't become concentrated the way they do on the stove. Compensate with spices and other flavor-boosters and you'll learn to love your Crock-Pot soups.

Lentil-Vegetable Soup

Serves 8

I created this recipe more than a decade ago when my daughter was a baby. It was the perfect nourishment when she was sick—hearty yet easy to digest. Some of my favorite ingredients in this soup are the kabocha and kale. The former lends a subtle touch of sweetness and thickens the broth. (Folks who want more sweetness can add some honey.) The latter is a healthful dark, leafy green that adds great color and texture and holds up well to reheating. Beyond that, add or replace any vegetables you want.

1/2 cup split peas
8 cups water
1/2 cup red lentils (or any other type of lentil)
3 tablespoons olive oil, divided
1 large onion, large diced
1 cup kabocha, half small dice, half diced
1 bunch kale, sliced into strips, with stems chopped into small
    pieces and separated from leaves
1 tablespoon rock salt, or to taste
1 tablespoon garlic powder
1/2 finger ginger, smashed
2 bay leaves
1 (14.5-ounce) can vegetable or chicken broth
1 medium zucchini, quartered and sliced about 2-inches thick
2 stalks celery, chopped
1 (14.5-ounce) can diced tomatoes (optional)
1 to 2 tablespoons honey, or to taste (optional)

Place split peas in pot with water and 1 tablespoon of the oil. Seal pot and bring to pressure. Lower heat and cook 7 minutes, then quick-release pressure.

Add lentils, seal pot, and bring to pressure. Lower heat and cook 5 minutes. Take pot off heat and allow natural-pressure release.

Use hand mixer in pot to partially blend soup. Or remove two-thirds of peas and lentils to blender and blend, then return to pot.

Add onions, small-diced kabocha, kale stems, salt, garlic powder, ginger, bay leaves, and broth. Seal lid, bring to pressure, lower heat, and cook 1 minute. Quick-release pressure.

Add kale leaves, remaining kabocha, zucchini, celery, and diced tomatoes if using. Seal lid again, bring to pressure, lower heat, and cook another minute. Quick-release pressure under running tap.

Add honey if using, mix, and taste. Adjust seasoning if necessary. Add remaining 2 tablespoons olive oil. Mix into soup and serve.

Soon Doo Bu
(Korean Tofu Stew)

Serves 4

After deciding I wanted a recipe for Korean tofu stew in this collection, I didn't have to think twice about whom to ask: local cooking instructor Walter Rhee, who's gained a following for his Asian cooking classes and Chinatown food tours. (Visit www. waltereatshawaii.com.) I'm excited to include this dish because it calls for authentic Korean ingredients such as gochu garu (Korean pepper flakes) and myul-chi (large dried Korean anchovies). These items aren't readily available in supermarkets; instead, go to Korean grocers such as Keeaumoku and Palama markets. The proper way of serving soon doo bu, says Rhee, is to ladle it over rice in the style of a loco moco.

2 tablespoons vegetable oil

2-1/2 cups chopped kim chee, squeezed to remove liquid

2 to 3 fresh shucked oysters, quick-rinsed in fresh water (optional)

1 stalk finely chopped green onion

1/2 tablespoon minced garlic

1/4 pound julienned pork

1/2 teaspoon sea salt

1/2 teaspoon sesame oil

1/2 teaspoon ground black pepper

1-1/2 tablespoons gochu garu (Korean red pepper flakes)

3 cups stock

1 block soft tofu

1 tablespoon flour mixed with 1/2 cup cold water

1 egg

Stock:
1/2 cup myul-chi (Korean dried large size anchovies)
1/3 cup daikon chunks
1/4 cup dried shiitake mushrooms
1 (2 x 2-inch) piece konbu
4 cups water

Make stock first: Combine all ingredients in pressure cooker. Seal lid, bring to pressure on high, reduce heat and cook 5 minutes. Quick-release pressure, strain stock, and discard solids. Set aside.

In pot on medium heat, add cooking oil and stir-fry kim chee, oysters if using, green onion, garlic, pork, salt, sesame oil, pepper, and gochu garu, until pork is cooked.

Add stock and bring to boil, then add tofu, whole or broken into pieces. Bring pot to boil again.

Add flour mixture to thicken soup; bring to boil. Crack raw egg into soup before serving.

Creamy Curried Butternut Soup

Serves 8

Despite the coconut milk and the creamy texture it creates, this is a light soup that can be made entirely vegan. It's a nice break from the often heavy, meaty dishes typical of slow cooking.

2 pound butternut squash, cut in 8 pieces, peeled and seeded
2 cups vegetable or chicken broth or stock
1 cup diced onion
4 cloves garlic, smashed and minced
2 tablespoons grated ginger, with juice
1 (4-ounce) can coconut milk
1 to 2 tablespoons Thai red curry paste (available in Asian section of most supermarkets)
1 tablespoon lime juice
1/2 cup chopped cilantro

Combine squash, broth, onion, garlic, and ginger in 6- or 7-quart slow cooker. Cook on low 6 hours, until squash is very tender. Use an immersion wand to purée soup in the crock, or mash with a potato masher.

Stir in coconut milk, curry paste, and lime juice. Taste, adding more curry paste or lime if desired. Let cook another 30 minutes to heat through. Serve garnished with cilantro.

{ Veggies & Sides }

S ide dishes can make a main dish shine or they can stand on their own as a light meal. The following array of pressure cooker dishes illustrates the many ways the appliance lends efficiency to preparation.

In making taro cake, the cooker saves time every step of the way in a dish that usually takes an investment of many hours. Miso Eggplant, meanwhile, can be turned around in a fraction of an hour. Cauliflower Casserole demonstrates how pressure cooking can serve as one step in a larger preparation process.

A nd don't discount the slow cooker for making side dishes. Because slow cooking involves such an investment in time, we tend to think of it as useful for main dishes only. If something's going to take six-hours-plus to come to fruition it had better be the main act, right?

There are times when a hearty vegetable dish or a nice stuffing will help round out a meal when the entree is being baked, stir-fried, roasted, or grilled. The fact that it can be cooking away while you shop, clean up and/or prep the main dish is a bonus.

Taro Cake

Serves 8

I found so many variations of this dish it made my head spin. Most called for rice and tapioca flours, which I thought might be humbug for some folks. So after more poking around, I hit upon a few recipes that utilize regular white flour. The version I put together will appeal to local palates with shiitake mushroom, dried shrimp and the always-ono lup cheong. Incidentally, the pressure cooker is a perfect vehicle for cooking taro, cutting a couple of hours of cooking time down to about 40 minutes. This two-part recipe starts with that process, and then follows with combining the ingredients and steaming the cake in the cooker. In about an hour's time, you've got a hearty taro cake.

2 cups taro (about 1 softball-sized corm), cooked and diced into large cubes

1 cup flour

3/4 cup water

2 teaspoons soy sauce

1 tablespoon sherry

2 teaspoons sesame oil

1 tablespoon garlic powder

1 teaspoon salt

2 lup cheong sausage links, thinly sliced

4 large shiitake mushrooms, soaked in water, stems removed and large diced

1/2 cup dried shrimp, cut into small pieces

3/4 cup sliced green onion

First, cook the taro: Wearing gloves, cut off skin of corm. Rinse and cut into several chunks. Place in pressure cooker with 3/4 to 1 cup of water. Secure lid, bring to pressure, lower heat and cook about 40 minutes. Quick-release pressure and open lid. Taste taro to ensure it's fully cooked (if your mouth feels itchy, taro is not fully cooked.)

When taro is done, cool slightly then large dice. Set aside.

In large bowl, combine flour and water and mix well. Add soy sauce, sherry, sesame oil, garlic powder, and salt; combine well.

Add taro, lup cheong, mushrooms, shrimp, and green onion. Combine well.

Place taro cake mixture in a 7-inch round casserole dish or glass bowl.

Add 1 cup water to pressure cooker, place trivet in pot, and place foil strips (see page 8) on trivet. These will be used to retrieve bowl from pot when taro cake is cooked. Set dish on foil strips. Tuck in strips, seal lid, bring pot to pressure on high, lower heat, and cook 15 minutes.

Allow natural-pressure release for 5 minutes, then quick-release pressure. Remove dish carefully using foil strips. Cool for a few minutes, then slice taro cake into pieces and serve.

Slow-Simmered Kabocha

Kabocha, sometimes called Japanese pumpkin, is my favorite vegetable to make in the slow cooker, so easily done it's just silly. This recipe uses homemade dashi, the making of which is a good basic technique to know. If you don't want to bother, though, use 2 cups chicken or vegetable broth.

Serve it as a side dish or make it a vegetarian meal with a serving of rice. One serving is incredibly low in calories and other bad things.

1 small kabocha squash, about 2 pounds
2 tablespoons mirin
1 tablespoon sugar
1 tablespoon soy sauce
1 teaspoon slivered ginger

Dashi
2-inch square piece konbu (available in Asian markets)
2 cups water
1/2 cup bonito flakes (available in Asian markets)

To make dashi: Place konbu and water in small pot over medium heat. When bubbles just begin to form around konbu, turn off heat. Remove konbu and set aside. Add bonito to water and let steep about 5 minutes. Strain.

Scrub kabocha well; cut in wedges and remove seeds. Do not peel. Place in 4- to 6-quart slow cooker.

Add mirin, soy sauce, and sugar to dashi broth. Stir to

dissolve sugar, then pour over kabocha.

Cut reserved konbu into strips and sprinkle over kabocha. Cook 4 hours on low, until very soft.

Serve with cooking liquid.

{ BASIC ROAST KABOCHA }

Brush wedges of kabocha with olive oil; sprinkle with salt and pepper. Pile into slow cooker and cook on low 3 to 4 hours, until tender but not too soft. Even a small kabocha makes a lot, which can be used many ways. Eat as is, or slice it for salads or to add to stir-fries or soups.

TIPS FOR CUTTING A KABOCHA

- Use the point of a knife to make a shallow cut into the kabocha near the bottom stem. Secure the widest part of the blade in the cut, press down, and rock back and forth until the kabocha splits.
- Use a paring knife to cut around the stem (this requires good wrist strength). Once you get a chunk out, switch to a bigger knife and cut wedges starting from the hole you just made.
- Position a cleaver just to the side of the stem and hit the cleaver with a mallet.
- Put the whole beast in the microwave on high about 3 minutes. The skin will then be soft enough to pierce.

Steamed Whole Artichokes with Sriracha Sauce

Serves 8

As a party dish, quartered artichokes offer a light alternative to the usual chip-and-dip appetizers. The segments make ideal finger food, each piece comprising a section of the heart and several leaves.

Four artichokes fit nicely in an oval pot at least 6 quarts in size. If you have a smaller round pot, you could make a single 'choke just for yourself.

4 large artichokes
12 garlic cloves
1 cup white wine (or water)
Juice of 1 lemon

Dip:
1/4 cup mayonnaise
1 teaspoon Thai chili sauce (sriracha)

Cut off stems and tough outer leaves of each artichoke. Slice 1 inch off the top and cut off thorny leaf tips. Separate leaves slightly, rinse and drain well. Stand in slow cooker. Tuck garlic cloves among the leaves. Pour wine and lemon juice around artichokes. Cook on low 4 hours. To test for doneness, pull a leaf from the base of one artichoke; it should release easily.

To make dip: Combine mayonnaise and sriracha. Taste and add more chili sauce if desired.

When artichokes have cooled slightly, cut each one in quarters. Scoop out bristley choke and tiny inside leaves. The flesh will have a nice, lemony flavor.

Presentation is everything: Place dip in a bowl in center of round serving dish and arrange artichoke quarters around it like petals.

SLOW COOKING VEGETABLES

Think of your slow cooker as a miniature oven. Anything that takes about an hour to roast in an oven will do well in a slow cooker—whole root vegetables such as beets or potatoes, for example. Let them go on low for 4 to 6 hours (don't add any liquid), and they will essentially roast their way to tenderness.

{ Enter the Entrée }

L ocal fare has always been diverse. Think stuffed bittermelon versus chicken luau versus miso pork. But today, that variety is expanded even further to encompass the upscale (Braised Abalone with Daikon) and the creative reimagining of classic dishes (Vegetarian Oden). In all cases, preparation in the pressure cooker delivers efficiency and boosted flavor.

T he best way to use a slow cooker to make workaday life easier is to cook on the weekends and reheat on the weekdays. But I know, I know. What you want your slow cooker to do is make dinner while you're at work. This is the holy grail of slow cooking, and I'm sorry to say, not all recipes are conducive to cooking for nine or 10 hours.

That said, the holy grail is attainable. Some beef or pork dishes, especially those involving large cuts, can go for eight to 10 hours, and some bean dishes for 12.

Chicken Papaya

Serves 4 to 6

Having grown up with Japanese-influenced home cooking, I enjoy a squash stir-fry: kabocha with pork or aburage, long squash and chicken. It is the latter that this Filipino dish most reminds me of, but chicken papaya is much more flavorful with its aromatic green papaya and punches of patis and fresh ginger. The dish is cooked in two stages: chicken first, then papaya is added to the pot. Total cooking time is about 30 minutes.

1 tablespoon olive oil
2 pounds bone-in chicken thighs, skin and fat removed
1 onion, large dice
2 cups water
1 (14.5-ounce) can chicken broth
2-1/2 tablespoons patis
2 teaspoons garlic powder
1 finger ginger, peeled and smashed
2 teaspoons salt, or to taste
1/2 bunch marungay leaves (about 3 cups)
4 pounds green papaya

Heat oil in pot, brown chicken and onions, about 5 minutes.

Add water, broth, patis, garlic powder, ginger, and salt. Mix, seal lid, bring pot to pressure on high, lower heat, and cook 12 minutes.

Meanwhile, rinse marungay, pluck from stalks, and set aside.

Rinse papaya, slice off ends and halve lengthwise. Scoop out seeds, then peel off skin with vegetable peeler. Slice into 2-inch chunks.

Remove pot from heat and quick-release pressure. Add papaya and marungay. Quickly mix, seal lid and bring to pressure again. Lower heat and cook 8 minutes. Quick-release and check papaya for doneness. It should be very tender.

If papaya needs to be cooked further, cook under pressure 2 more minutes, then quick-release pressure.

If you like, remove chicken from pot, shred meat and return to pot, discarding bones. Stir and serve.

Nishime

Serves 8

For Japanese families, there's no party fare more standard than nishime. Crafting a nishime recipe for the pressure cooker takes some know-how, given that some ingredients are rather delicate for this style of cooking. But leave it to chef Grant Sato to figure it out, then graciously share his expertise.

- 1 package dried konbu (sold in Asian section of supermarkets)
- 1 pound gobo, cut into obliques (cut crosswise at an angle)
- 1 package konnyaku, cut into triangles (available in refrigerated section near fresh tofu)
- 4 pieces dried shiitake mushrooms, soaked, stemmed and cut into bite-size pieces
- 1/3 pound fresh hasu (lotus root), peeled and cut into 1/4-inch slices
- 8 cups dashi (Japanese stock, made from powder sold in Asian section of supermarkets)

continued on the next page

1/2 cup soy sauce
1/2 cup brown sugar
1 pound chicken or pork, cut into 1-inch strips
1 carrot, cut into obliques
1 can bamboo shoots, cut into 1-inch strips
1 pound araimo (Japanese taro), peeled and cut into 1-inch cubes

---

Soak dried konbu until hydrated and pliable. Tie into 8 knots about 3 inches apart, then cut between knots. Set aside.

In pot, place gobo, konnyaku, shiitake, hasu, dashi, soy sauce, and brown sugar. Seal lid, bring to pressure on high, lower heat and cook 10 minutes.

Quick-release pressure and add meat, carrots, konbu knots, bamboo shoots, and araimo. Simmer uncovered for 15 minutes. Taste and add more soy sauce if necessary.

Chinese Chicken Curry Hot Pot

Serves 6

Newspaper reader Melissa Pang Nikaido sent me the recipe for a family favorite, a chicken curry with bold flavors of ginger, curry, and oyster sauce. I have adapted it with a few ingredients you might find in a Chinese hot pot. Foo chuk (dried bean curd), dried shiitake mushrooms, cubes of fried tofu, and taro are easily found in Asian grocery stores, and the results are well worth the effort.

8 bone-in skinless chicken thighs

12 ounces taro, peeled and cubed

10 dried shiitake mushrooms, soaked in hot water to soften

4 sticks foo chuk (dried bean curd), soaked in hot water to soften

1 block (6 ounces) fried tofu, or aburage, soaked in hot water to remove excess oil, cut in squares

3 stalks green onion, for garnish

Seasonings:

1 tablespoon minced garlic

2-inch piece ginger, peeled and cut in slivers

2 to 3 tablespoons curry powder

1 tablespoon sugar

1/4 cup sherry or red wine

1 cup chicken broth

1/4 cup oyster sauce

continued on the next page

Measure seasonings into crock and mix. Add chicken and taro; turn to coat pieces. Squeeze mushrooms, foo chuk, and tofu to remove excess water. Add to crock. Cook on low about 5 hours, until chicken and taro are tender. Stir halfway through if possible.

Top with green onion before serving.

{ TO REDUCE FAT } Remove chicken and other items from liquid in crock. Skim fat from liquid. (To make a thicker gravy, dissolve 1/4 cup tapioca starch in 1/4 cup water and stir into liquid; turn heat to high for a few minutes. This may also be done in a pot on the stove.) Return everything to the pot. (For ease of eating, chicken can be deboned first.)

Tips for slow cooking chicken:

- For best results, use bone-in chicken pieces, but remove the skin (this cuts oiliness). Thighs have the most flavor and are easy to slice for easy serving or for the most compact storage of leftovers. White meat tends to dry out.
- The biggest mistake people make when slow cooking chicken is overcooking. In most slow cookers, chicken will be done in just over four hours, although it can go longer for added tenderness. Don't let it cook too long, though, or the texture may turn dry and mealy.

Spicy Honey-Garlic Wings

Serves 4 to 6

SLOW

Chicken wings are such tiny bits of meat, it's easy to infuse them with flavor. Cooking them in the slow cooker leaves them tender and tasty, but pale. A quick run under the broiler crisps the skin and gives them a delicious-looking tan.

4 pounds chicken wings
1/4 cup sesame oil
2 tablespoons sesame seeds
2 tablespoons chopped green onion

Sauce:
1/4 cup soy sauce
1/4 cup mirin
1/4 cup honey
2 tablespoons grated ginger, with juice
4 large cloves garlic, minced
1 teaspoon Thai chili sauce (sriracha), or more to taste

Combine sauce ingredients in 6- or 7-quart slow cooker; stir well. Add chicken wings and toss to coat. Cook on low 4 hours, until cooked through.

Arrange wings on rimmed cooking sheet. Brush with sesame oil and sprinkle with sesame seeds. Broil until nicely browned, 5 to 10 minutes. Sprinkle with green onions.

Galbi Jim
(Korean Short Rib and Pear Stew)

Serves 6

Kathleen Freitas, who regularly pressure cooks her meals at home, shares this recipe, a favorite because she loves the combination of pears with soy sauce and mirin, which produce a mellow sweet-sour flavor. Kathleen chops her pear into cubes because she enjoys the added texture but says you can grate the pear if you like. This allows the fruit to dissolve into the sauce.

2 pounds beef short ribs
5 large dried shiitake mushrooms, soaked, stems
    removed and thinly sliced
1/2 Asian pear, peeled, cored and cut into 1/2-
    inch cubes
2 carrots, peeled and cut into 1-inch pieces
2 tablespoons mirin
1/4 cup soy sauce
1 tablespoon brown sugar
1/4 cup thinly sliced green onion
2 cloves garlic, peeled and chopped,
    or 1 tablespoon garlic powder
Ground black pepper, to taste
1 cup water

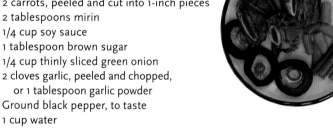

Combine all ingredients in pot and mix until incorporated. Seal lid, bring to pressure on high, then lower heat and cook 45 minutes.

Remove from heat and allow natural-pressure release for 15 minutes. Quick-release pressure and serve.

Local Style Curry

Serves 6

This recipe can be whipped up within 30 minutes from start to finish, since cooking time for a beef version is about 16 minutes (plus 10-minute natural-pressure release) or a mere 8 minutes if you use chicken. It's a natural for the weeknight recipe rotation.

1 tablespoon cooking oil
1 onion, chopped
3 pounds beef, cut into 1-inch thick cubes*
2 (14.5-ounce) cans beef or chicken broth
2 bay leaves
1/4 cup curry powder
1 tablespoon garlic powder
1-1/2 teaspoons salt
2 large potatoes, cut into 1-inch chunks
2 carrots, cut into 1-inch chunks
3 celery stalks, cut into 2-inch pieces
2 tablespoons cornstarch dissolved in 2 tablespoons water

In pressure cooker pot, heat oil and sauté onions, about 2 minutes. Add beef and brown.

Add broth, bay leaves, curry powder, garlic powder, and salt. Seal lid, bring to pressure on high, lower heat, and cook 12 minutes. Naturally release pressure for 10 minutes, then quick-release if necessary.

Add potatoes, carrots, and celery. Seal lid, bring to pressure, lower heat, and cook another 4 minutes. Remove from

heat and quick-release, then open lid and return pot to burner on medium. Curry should be simmering.

Stir cornstarch mixture, then add to curry and stir while thickening. Simmer 5 minutes and serve.

{ * } Beef can be replaced with boneless chicken breast or thighs. Add vegetables along with chicken, then cook at pressure for 4 minutes, plus 4-minute natural release. Quick-release, then proceed with thickening gravy.

Kare-Kare Oxtail Stew

Serves 8 to 10

Kare-kare, or kari-kari, is a Filipino oxtail stew made with peanut butter. This version capitalizes on the slow cooker's ability to make an excellent stock, which serves as the basis for the stew's gravy.

Ground rice and achiote are traditionally used to thicken the stew and color it a pale orange, but if you'd rather simplify, use cornstarch or tapioca starch for thickening and live with the natural beige tone.

3 to 4 pounds oxtails
1 medium onion, sliced
2 cloves garlic, crushed
1 quart water
1 pound green beans, sliced into 2-inch lengths
3 small eggplant, sliced into 1-inch wedges
2 teaspoons achiote powder, sold in small packets near Filipino
    seasonings in Asian markets and some supermarkets
1/2 cup chunky peanut butter
1/2 cup toasted ground rice (see note)
1 teaspoon fish sauce

Place oxtails, onions, and garlic in 6- to 7-quart with water, adding a little more if needed just to cover oxtails. Cook on low 6 hours, or until meat is tender. Remove oxtails and onions. Strain stock and skim fat. Refrigerate oxtails and onions.

Return stock to pot; add beans, and eggplant. Cook on low 3 to 4 hours, until vegetables are tender. Stir in achiote powder, peanut butter, and ground rice, stirring to combine. Return oxtails and onions to pot. Continue cooking until oxtails are heated through and mixture is thickened. Drizzle with fish sauce.

{ VARIATIONS }
Eggplant and beans are typically found in this dish, but other vegetables can be used, including greens such as bok choy, added at the end of the cooking time.

{ NOTE } To make ground rice, toast uncooked rice over medium heat in a dry skillet until golden. Grind in a coffee-grinder.

Hearty Poi Stew

*Poi is a great way to thicken cooking liquids and create a creamy
gravy. It's also a nutritional improvement over cornstarch, packing
protein, fiber, and other good things—whereas cornstarch is just,
well, starch.*

2 pounds boneless beef short ribs, in 1-inch cubes
2 tablespoons soy sauce
2 teaspoons red pepper flakes
8 large cloves garlic, crushed and chopped
1 large onion, in wedges
2 cups potatoes, taro, or sweet potatoes in chunks
2 carrots, in 1-inch pieces, about 1-1/2 cups
1 red bell pepper, diced
1 sprig rosemary
1 (14-ounce) can diced tomatoes (or 2 cups fresh)
1-1/2 cups beef broth
1/2 cup red wine
1 cup poi

Place beef in a 6- or 7-quart slow cooker. Toss with soy
sauce and pepper flakes. Add remaining ingredients except
poi. Cook on low 6 to 8 hours, until meat is tender.

Skim fat from pot (tilting the crock makes this easier). Stir
in poi and let cook 30 minutes longer, until gravy thickens.

{ OPTIONAL FIRST STEP } Beef can be browned before adding to pot, along with garlic and onions. This boosts the beef flavor and allows the aromatics to "bloom."

{ THINK GREEN } Add some color to the pot by stirring in some sliced kale, baby bok choy or 2-inch pieces of choy sum into the stew at the same time as the poi. Greens cook quickly and will keep their bright color when added at the end of cooking time.

{ VARIATION } Bone-in beef shanks also work well. Debone and slice the meat after cooking for easier eating.

FAST

Kālua Pig

Serves 8

My first attempt at pressure cooking was executing this recipe, posted on the Tasty Island food blog by Pomai Souza. The post chronicled Souza's misadventures in arriving at a successful kālua pig recipe for the pressure cooker. (Actually, it's more procedure than recipe.) I followed Souza's directives and produced a wonderfully moist, flavorful, and fool-proof kālua pig, all within 2 hours. Here, I pass on Souza's knowledge with my approximations for a formal recipe. Adjust as you see fit. For visuals and his take on the process, visit Souza's blog at http://tastyislandhawaii.com/2011/04/03/pressure-cooked-kalua-pig/

6 ti leaves, stems removed
5-pound pork butt with a generous fat cap
1/8 cup Hawaiian salt, or to taste
3 tablespoons liquid smoke, or to taste
2 cups water

Wash ti leaves and set aside to dry.

Deeply score pork and rub in salt and liquid smoke on each side of roast. Place into pressure cooker pot fat side up. Pour water into side of pot. Line sides of pot and cover top of roast with more ti leaves. (Do not line bottom of pot with leaves—it will scorch.)

Seal lid, bring to pressure on high, lower heat and cook 1-1/2 hours. Turn off heat and leave on burner. Allow natural-pressure release, about 30 minutes.

Release lid and check for doneness. Pork should fall apart and shred easily with a fork. If necessary, cook under pressure an additional 15 minutes. Allow natural-pressure release. Release lid and taste, adjusting seasoning as necessary.

Remove pork and shred. Reserve liquid in pot and pour over kālua pig when serving to enhance juiciness.

Portuguese Sausage Chili

Serves 6

*Ever since I got my pressure cooker, I've been experimenting
with different chili recipes and spices. I've learned that cumin
and cinnamon added to chili powder provide a winning depth
of flavor. I've concocted this sweeter chili using kabocha, which
also adds sweetness and thickness to the sauce, along with some
pineapple jelly. Add to the pot spicy Portuguese sausage and it's
a perfect match. For more heat, up the chili powder; amp it up
further with dried crushed red pepper or cayenne.*

1 cup dry black beans
1 cup dry navy beans
4-1/2 cups water, divided
1 tablespoon oil
1 (8- or 10-ounce) Portuguese sausage, casing removed, diced
1/2 package bacon, sliced crosswise into 1/2-inch strips, diced
1 large onion, diced
1 cup kabocha, diced into 1/2-inch pieces
2 tablespoons pineapple jelly
2 teaspoons salt, or to taste
3 tablespoons chili powder, or to taste
2 tablespoons cumin
1/4 teaspoon ground cinnamon
1/2 teaspoon cayenne pepper or 1 tablespoon dried crushed
    red pepper (optional)
2 (15-ounce) cans tomato sauce
2 (14.5-ounce) cans diced tomatoes

Rinse beans, then place in pressure cooker with 4 cups of water and oil. Seal lid, bring to pressure, lower heat, and cook 22 minutes. Remove pot from heat and allow pressure to release naturally, about 15 more minutes.

Drain beans and set aside.

In pot, fry sausage and drain on paper towel. Set aside.

Fry bacon and onions in pot, then drain on paper towel. Drain out three quarters of oil.

Return bacon and onions to pot. Add remaining water, kabocha, pineapple jelly, salt, and spices. Mix well.

Add tomato sauce and diced tomatoes to pot. Do not stir.

Seal lid, bring pot to pressure, reduce heat, and cook 3 minutes. Quick-release pressure.

Return beans and sausage to the pot and stir. Cover but do not seal lid and simmer 5 to 10 minutes.

Stuffed Bittermelon with Black Bean Sauce

Serves 3 to 4

This classic Chinese favorite is usually enjoyed at a restaurant or a party if you're lucky enough to have an aunty willing to pull it together. It does take time to hollow out the bittermelon pieces, mix the pork filling and stuff it into the vegetable. But in the pressure cooker, it's a short wait from the time the morsels hit the pot to when they're served. And the end product is so perfectly cooked, and the flavors so well infused, it's well worth the effort. You'll probably return to this recipe again and again. I know I have.

2 medium bittermelon, cut crosswise into 2-inch pieces and hollowed out in the center
3/4 cup water

Pork filling:
3/4 pound ground pork
3 tablespoons minced water chestnuts
3 tablespoons shiitake mushroom, soaked, stemmed, and minced
2 tablespoons minced green onions
1/2 teaspoon salt
1/4 teaspoon pepper
1/2 teaspoon sesame oil
1 teaspoon soy sauce
1 teaspoon cooking sherry

Black bean sauce:

1-1/2 tablespoons fermented black beans, rinsed and mashed
2 tablespoons minced garlic
2 tablespoons white wine
3/4 cup chicken broth
1 tablespoon sesame oil or aji sesame oil
1 tablespoon soy sauce
1 tablespoon oyster sauce

Par-cook bittermelon: Add water to pressure cooker pot, insert steamer basket, place bittermelon pieces in basket. Seal lid, bring to pressure on high heat, lower heat and cook 1 minute. Quick-release pressure. Remove pieces and let cool. Remove basket.

In bowl, mix all ingredients for pork filling and stuff bittermelon pieces. Place in pot.

In small bowl, combine black bean sauce ingredients, mix well, and pour over stuffed bittermelon. Seal lid, bring to pressure, lower heat, and cook 1 minute. Release pressure, open lid, and check if pork filling is cooked. If necessary, cook under pressure another minute. Release pressure, then simmer 5 minutes.

Miso Pork

Serves 6 to 8

There's such great return for such little effort from this recipe for a local classic. The flavor is incredible, and because the pressure cooker delivers so quickly, it's easy to pull off this roast for a weeknight dinner. I used a combo of red and white miso because the red offers an earthy flavor, while the white contributes a mellower sweetness. But feel free to use just one type. Be creative with leftovers: fill burritos and quesadillas, top pizzas, shred and top with pickles for sliders, or cube meat and stir-fry with veggies.

5 pounds pork butt, cut into quarters
1/2 cup white miso
1/4 cup red miso
3/4 cup soy sauce
1/2 cup brown sugar
1 finger ginger, peeled and crushed
2 teaspoons garlic powder
1/4 cup sake

Place pork in pot.

Combine miso, soy sauce, sugar, ginger, garlic powder, and sake. Mix, then pour over pork.

Seal lid, and on high heat bring to pressure. Lower heat and cook 40 minutes. Allow natural-pressure release, then check tenderness of pork. It should be soft enough to tear with a fork. If necessary, cook under pressure another 10 minutes.

If you like, finish off the roast in the broiler to char the miso sauce. Broil 3 to 5 minutes.

Hoisin-Guava Baby Back Ribs

Serves 6

Ribs are perfect for the slow cooker. Made tender and flavorful through long, slow cooking, they're usually prepared in an oven, on a grill, or in a smoker. It can be high-maintenance. A Crock-Pot version will take hours, but you don't even have to be in the building.

You could do without the broiling and glazing at the end—but if you take the trouble you will be so much happier.

5 to 6 pounds pork baby back ribs
Pepper, to taste
2 tablespoons cornstarch dissolved in 1/4 cup water

Sauce:
1 (8.5 ounce) jar hoisin sauce, about 1 cup
1 (10-ounce) jar guava jelly
1/4 cup red wine, dry sherry or whisky
2-inch piece ginger, peeled, smashed, and minced, about 1/4 cup
6 cloves garlic, minced
2 teaspoons red pepper flakes

Season ribs with pepper and stand upright around sides of a 6-quart slow cooker. Meaty sides should face outward, with the thicker part of the ribs at the bottom. Overlap slabs if necessary.

Combine sauce ingredients, pour over ribs. Cook on low until tender, 6 to 8 hours. Ribs should not be so soft that the meat is falling off the bone.

Place ribs on a greased broiling rack, meaty side down. Preheat broiler.

Skim fat from liquid in slow cooker; strain 2 cups into saucepan over medium heat. Stir in cornstarch slurry, and simmer until thickened.

Brush ribs with thickened sauce and broil until beginning to brown, 2 to 4 minutes. Turn ribs, brush with more sauce and broil until well browned and sticky, about 10 minutes longer. Brush with more sauce occasionally.

Let rest 5 minutes. Slice ribs; serve with extra sauce.

{ EASY DOES IT } The simplest approach to slow cooker ribs relies on store-bought barbecue sauce. I like the Spicy Hawaiian Bar-B-Q Sauce from Noh Foods. Stand ribs around the crock, squeeze the juice from 1 lemon over ribs, followed by most of a bottle of sauce (save some). Once cooked, ribs can be broiled and glazed with extra sauce. Or serve them straight from the crock, with sauce for dipping.

Sweet-Sour Pig's Feet

Serves 6

This tangy, hearty dish is often served to new mothers as a way of restoring strength in the days after childbirth. Others crave it for its simple, puckery chewiness. Be sure to serve the slices of ginger with the meat—they will be tender, mellow, and a delicious complement.

3 pounds pig's feet
1 pound ginger, in thin slices
1 pound wong tong (see notes), broken in pieces
1 cup black vinegar (see notes)
1/2 cup white or cider vinegar

Bring large pot of water to boil and parboil pig's feet about 10 minutes, then rinse and drain to remove impurities. Place in 6- or 7-quart slow cooker. Arrange ginger and wong tong pieces around pig's feet. Pour vinegar over all. Cook on low about 8 hours. Taste juices and add more vinegar if desired. Remove everything from pot except liquid. Skim fat from juices. Spoon juices over meat.

{ OPTIONAL ADDITIONS } 1 cup raw peanuts, shelled; 6 hard-cooked eggs, peeled; 8 to 10 whole dried shiitake mushrooms, soaked and squeezed dry; 1 large bunch dark Chinese greens (such as bok choy or mustard cabbage), in 2-inch segments. Peanuts should be stirred in at the beginning of cooking, eggs and mushrooms in the last 1 to 2 hours, greens at the very end (lay on top and let steam).

{ **IF MAKING AHEAD** } Refrigerate meat separately from juices. Before heating, remove fat from top of juices and bring juices to simmer in saucepan over medium heat, thickening if desired with a mixture of cornstarch or tapioca starch and water. Place meat and ginger slices in sauce to warm.

{ **VARIATION** } My mother makes this with fresh ham shanks instead of feet. The pieces tend to be more uniform in size.

{ **INGREDIENT NOTES** } Wong tong (slabs of Chinese brown sugar) and black vinegar (an inky vinegar derived from rice) can be found in Chinatown markets, Asian markets, and some supermarkets.

Tofu Casserole

Serves 6

This rich, almost custardy dish has become my new comfort food. It's versatile—feel free to replace pork and shrimp with bite-size pieces of chicken, and omit or add any veggies that you like. Remember, however, that shiitake adds lots of flavor, so it's an ingredient that goes a long way. A note: drain tofu as thoroughly as possible. Even with hours-long draining in the refrigerator, my cooked casserole had excessive liquid. I drained off about half of it, but as the liquid was well flavored, I kept the rest to pour over my rice when I ate the dish.

1/4 pound ground pork
1/4 pound shrimp, large diced
3 shiitake mushrooms, soaked, stems removed and large diced
1 cup sliced green onion
1 medium carrot, julienned
4 ounces (1/2 can) bamboo shoot strips
4 ounces (1/2 can) sliced water chestnuts, cut into thirds
1 egg
1/4 cup panko
1 tablespoon grated or minced ginger
1-1/2 teaspoons sesame oil
2 teaspoons garlic powder
1 teaspoon salt
Pepper, to taste
1 (20-ounce) block soft tofu, crumbled by hand into medium
    chunks and well drained

In large bowl, combine everything but tofu and mix well. Add tofu and gently combine. Transfer to 7-inch round glass bowl or casserole dish.

Fill pot with 1 cup water. Place trivet in pot. Place foil strips on trivet for retrieving dish later when casserole is cooked. To construct strips, see page 8. Tuck the ends into the pot, cover, and seal lid.

Bring pot to pressure on high, lower heat, and cook 15 minutes. Quick-release pressure. Untuck foil strips and carefully hoist dish from pot. There will be excess liquid. Drain if desired, or serve with casserole.

Ginger-Lime
Salmon Fillets

Serves 2

We tend to think of our slow cookers only in terms of hours of unattended cooking. But there are other ways this device can make a busy life an easier one. Let's say you have to take the kids to soccer practice at 4 p.m., or you want to go to a yoga class at 5, or you have to walk the dog precisely at 6.

A dish like this one with a shorter cooking time can be started just before you leave and be ready for serving when you get back, so that on these busy evenings you don't have to rely on takeout or rush around trying to assemble a meal in 20 minutes.

Gentle low heat produces a delicate, soft fillet, and the vibrant flavors in the sauce brighten the taste. This dish is simple, yet scores a high impact. I used salmon because it is easy to find year-round, but any firm-fleshed fish would work. If you luck into some nice swordfish or mahimahi from local waters, give it a try.

2 (8- to 10-ounce) salmon fillets
2 ti leaves, trimmed to fit slow cooker insert
Chopped green onion, slivered ginger and thin lime slices, for garnish

Marinade:
1 tablespoon grated ginger with juice
1 tablespoon fresh lime juice
2 tablespoons soy sauce
2 tablespoons sugar

Combine marinade ingredients, stirring to dissolve sugar, and pour over fish. Let marinate 30 minutes.

Remove fillets, and place on top of ti leaf in 5- to 7-quart slow cooker. Cover with second ti leaf. Pour marinade over fish. Cook on low 60 to 90 minutes, until salmon is cooked through (it should flake easily with a fork). Remove to serving dish. Spoon sauce from cooker over fish. Garnish as desired.

Liliko'i BBQ Beans

Serves 8

*These beans take their sweetness from liliko'i jelly, which can
be subbed with guava or the fruit flavor of your choice. It also
uses brewed coffee for balance, a tip I learned from* Slow Cooker
Revolution *by the editors of* Cook's Illustrated.

*This is a vegetarian dish, but you could easily stir in sausage
or diced ham and let it heat through for about 10 minutes.*

1 pound dry pinto beans
1 cup liliko'i (passion fruit) jelly
1/2 cup barbecue sauce
1/2 cup brewed coffee
1-1/2 cups chopped onion
4 cloves garlic, minced
1 cup chopped red bell pepper (in large chunks)
1/4 cup chopped cilantro
1 tablespoon minced fresh rosemary (or 1 teaspoon dried)
4 cups water

Combine ingredients in slow cooker. Cook on low 9 to 11
hours, until beans are tender.

Taste and adjust seasonings. Stir in more jelly or barbecue
sauce, or add mustard, chili pepper sauce, or brown sugar
as needed. Let sit about 10 minutes or hold on warm setting
for up to an hour to allow to thicken slightly (add hot water if
mixture becomes too thick).

{ NOTES } To shorten cooking time, beans may be cooked on
high setting in 5 to 7 hours, or soak overnight in cold water
before cooking.

Paniolo Chili

Serves 12

This is a slow-cooker version of my go-to chili recipe, which is in turn based on the first-place winner of the 1999 Great Hawaiian Chili Cookoff, by Jerry Hall of Ewa Beach. On the chili competition circuit, beans are frowned upon, but in my family it ain't chili without those beans, so my recipe includes them, without apology.

1-1/2 pounds boneless cross-rib roast, cut in 1/2-inch cubes
1 pound boneless pork butt, cut in 1/2-inch cubes
6 cloves garlic, crushed
1 large onion, diced
1/2 pound Portuguese sausage
1 large red bell pepper, diced
1 large green bell pepper, diced
2 cans kidney beans, with liquid
1/2 cup chili powder
1/4 cup cumin
2 cups chicken broth (or 1 15-ounce can)
1 (15-ounce) can tomato sauce
1 small red chile pepper, minced, or 1 teaspoon red pepper
   flakes

If desired, brown meat, garlic and onions lightly in a skillet with 2 tablespoons vegetable oil. If you'd rather not bother, just combine all the ingredients in a 6- or 7-quart slow cooker. Stir. Cook on low 4 to 6 hours, until meat is tender. Taste and adjust for spiciness.

Lasagna, Like Magic

Serves 8

*This was the recipe that restored my faith in my slow cooker.
Like magic it takes sauce, spices, and uncooked pasta noodles
and turns them into lasagna. First time I tried it, everything
went into the pot and we went to the movies. Came home to a
hot, chewy, gooey dinner.*

*Aha, said I, this is what a slow cooker is supposed to do. Make
life easier. So even though lasagna isn't really local-style food, I
include this recipe because it marked the beginning of my journey.*

1/2 pound ground turkey
1/2 pound (2 links) hot Italian sausage
1 cup chopped onion
2 cloves garlic, minced
1 (29-ounce) can tomato sauce
1 (6-ounce) can tomato paste
1 tablespoon fresh or 1 teaspoon dried oregano
1 tablespoon fresh or 1 teaspoon dried rosemary
1 pound nonfat cottage cheese
1 pound shredded mozzarella cheese
1 (13-ounce) box whole-wheat lasagna noodles, uncooked
1 small zucchini, thinly sliced
1 (10-ounce) package frozen chopped spinach, thawed and
    squeezed of all liquid
1/2 cup grated Parmesan cheese

Lightly brown ground turkey, sausage, onion, and garlic
(don't cook until well done or it will toughen in slow cooker).
Add tomato sauce, tomato paste, oregano, and rosemary. Stir
well, heating just long enough to warm sauce.

Combine cottage cheese and mozzarella.

Grease inside of a 6- or 7-quart slow cooker (see note).
Spoon about 1 cup meat sauce onto bottom of slow cooker,

covering well. Top with layer of uncooked noodles (break to fit, using small pieces to fill gaps). Top noodles with half of cheese mixture. Add more sauce, another layer of noodles and remaining cheese. Layer spinach and zucchini over top layer of cheese. Top with final layer of noodles. Pour remaining sauce over top. Sprinkle with Parmesan cheese. Cover and cook on low 4 hours or until noodles are tender. Turn off pot and remove cover for a few minutes to let noodles set.

{ NOTE } This recipe is designed for an oval slow cooker. If yours is round you probably will have more than 3 layers of noodles.

{ Desserts & Snacks }

D on't make the mistake of disregarding the pressure cooker for producing a diverse lineup of desserts and snacks. In less time than it will take you to assemble, measure and mix the ingredients, you can cook the vibrant sauce for an ono prune mui. Boiled peanuts are a breeze as well, with cooking time cut from the traditional hours of cooking to just 45 minutes. Bread pudding, rice pudding and puto are a snap as well.

D esserts made in a slow cooker deliver a fabulous element of surprise, as in "Look! I made this in my Crock-Pot," to which the likely response will be, "Really? Let me see that!" Slow cookers are great with recipes that normally call for a water bath, such as bread puddings and cheesecakes. They essentially act as an oven, producing quite impressive results while you're, say, taking a nap. And why not? Life is frantic enough. Let your slow cooker sweeten it a bit.

Jasmine Rice Pudding

Serves 6 to 8

The charm of this homey dessert is not only that it's versatile—it can be subtle and creamy or livened up with bits of flavorful dried fruit—but it requires very little effort for a pudding dish. Like most pressure cooker recipes, it overdelivers for the effort expended.

2-1/2 cups water
1 cup jasmine rice
1 tablespoon butter
1/4 teaspoon salt
1 (13.5-ounce) can coconut milk
1/3 cup brown sugar
Dried fruit such as cranberries or apricots; larger fruit should
   be slivered or diced (optional)
1 teaspoon vanilla
1 teaspoon cinnamon
1/4 teaspoon nutmeg
1/4 teaspoon allspice
Fresh fruit, sliced into small bites (optional)

Combine water, rice, butter, and salt in pressure cooker pot. Seal lid, bring to pressure on high, lower heat, and cook 8 minutes. Quick-release pressure under running tap.

Release lid and return pot to medium-high heat, and add coconut milk, sugar, and dried fruit if using. Bring to boil, stirring, then simmer uncovered about 4 to 6 minutes until consistency is like loose oatmeal. Add vanilla, spices, and fresh fruit if using.

Chinese Boiled Peanuts

Serves 4

Star-Advertiser reader Dorinda Won, an engineer from Alewa Heights, says she spent most of her life avoiding kitchen duty. But these days, she's taken to "dabbling" in cooking and baking, searching the Internet for interesting recipes and then creating her own version. That's how she came up with an original recipe for boiled peanuts that combines cinnamon with anise and cloves for a great aromatic backdrop, and it's become a family favorite. This adapted version is just a tad saltier.

1 pound raw peanuts in shell
1/4 cup dark soy sauce
3 tablespoons sugar
1/8 cup salt
1 (3-inch) stick cinnamon
2 star anise
5 cloves

Wash peanuts then soak in clean water for 30 minutes. Drain.

Place in pressure cooker with remaining ingredients. Add enough water to cover. Seal lid, bring to pressure on high heat, lower heat, and cook 45 minutes.

Quick-release pressure and check for doneness. If necessary, cook another 2 to 5 minutes. Quick-release pressure and let cool in pot. Drain liquid and serve.

Sweet Bread Pudding

Serves 6 to 8

This luscious dessert uses two local favorites, sweet bread and macadamia nuts, though you can swap them for any other type of bread or nut, and a variety of add-ins, including dried fruit or chocolate chips. The dessert is cooked in a 7-inch round glass bowl or casserole dish, which is placed on a trivet and foil strips. For details on this technique, see page 8.

1/2 cup sugar
1 tablespoon cinnamon
5 tablespoons butter, softened
8 to 12 slices sweet bread, cut into 2 x 4-inch pieces
3 large eggs
1-1/2 cup half-and-half
1/3 cup brown sugar
1/8 teaspoon salt
Diced macadamia nuts, for topping (optional)

In small bowl, combine sugar and cinnamon. Set aside.

Using some butter, grease inside and sides of glass bowl or casserole dish. Set aside.

Butter pieces of bread. Set aside.

In bowl, lightly whisk eggs. Whisk in half-and-half, brown sugar, and salt.

Coat bottom of casserole with 1/4 cup egg mixture. Place 4 to 6 pieces of bread into bowl. Pour about a third of egg mixture over bread. Sprinkle with cinnamon/sugar mixture.

Layer with more bread, more egg mixture and follow again with cinnamon/sugar. Repeat once more.

Fill pressure cooker with 2 cups water and place trivet inside pot. Place foil strips on trivet and put dish of bread pudding on top of strips. Secure lid, bring to pressure on high, and lower heat. Cook 20 to 25 minutes, depending on how much bread is packed into dish.

Remove pot from heat, allow pressure to come down naturally, about 10 minutes. Remove dish from pot using foil strips. Top with macadamia nuts.

If you want, you can brown the top of the bread pudding in a 350°F oven 5 to 10 minutes.

Puto

Serves 12

This Filipino steamed cake is usually served as mini cupcakes, but in the pressure cooker it's more practical to prepare in a 7-inch round casserole that fits nicely in the pot. There are countless versions of puto, some involving white flour and others using rice, and many incorporating coconut milk. This one is distinct in that it uses Bisquick, which produces a yellow cake rather than one that's snowy white. Though it may not look like classic puto, this version is nothing short of delicious and well worth the quick work it takes to make. It comes courtesy of family friends Joe and Sally Aguinaldo, whose Filipino dishes always delight.

1-1/4 cups Bisquick
6 ounces (1/2 of 12-ounce can) evaporated milk
3-1/2 ounces (1/4 of 14-ounce can) sweetened condensed milk
1/4 cup sugar
1 egg

Fill pressure cooker with 1 cup of water and insert trivet. Insert foil strips for removing casserole dish (see page 8). Grease 7-inch round casserole dish.

In bowl, whisk all ingredients together. Pour into casserole. Place casserole into pot on top of foil strips. Place dish on top of the strips. Tuck the ends of the strips into the pot, cover, and seal. On high heat, bring pot to pressure, then lower heat and steam puto for 16 minutes.

Quick-release pressure, open lid, and, using foil strips, remove casserole from pot. Test for doneness by inserting toothpick into center of puto; if it comes out clean, puto is done. If not, place foil strips and casserole back into pot, seal lid, bring pot to pressure, lower heat, and cook up to 3 additional minutes.

Remove casserole from pot, test for doneness. If thoroughly steamed, let puto cool for 20 minutes or so, then slice into 12 pieces and serve.

Prune Mui

Makes about 4 cups

When I tested this recipe, I added a small handful of li hing mui to the sauce before cooking, in hopes it would add some punch. After it was done, I tossed the sauce with the rest of the ingredients, tasted a prune—and cringed. The sauce tasted almost bitter with li hing flavor. I chalked it up as a learning experience and planned to retest the recipe again. But in the five days that the mui was set aside to merge and absorb flavors, the sharpness of the li hing assimilated nicely with the other elements for an assertive, yet rounded sauce. Success!

1 (10-ounce) package pitted prunes
1 (6-ounce) package dried apricots
4 ounces dried mango (about 1/2 medium package), sliced into thin strips
2 ounces dried cranberries (about 1/2 small package)
2 ounces lemon peel (about 1/2 small package), sliced into strips
2 ounces seedless li hing mui (about 1/2 small package), sliced in half

Sauce:

1/2 cup brown sugar
1 tablespoon rock salt
1 tablespoon cooking sherry, whiskey or rum
1/3 teaspoon Chinese five-spice powder
4 whole cloves
1/2 cup fresh lemon juice
Small handful seedless li hing mui

To make sauce, combine all ingredients. Place in pressure cooker, seal lid, and bring to pressure on high. Lower pressure and cook 6 minutes. Remove from heat, quick-release pressure, and cool.

Add dried fruit and crack seed, stir well.

Place in container and store on cool counter for 4 to 5 days, inverting container daily to redistribute sauce.

Mango Crisp
with Mac-Nut Topping

Serves 10

The slow cooker is a perfect tool for making fruit fillings for pies, layer cakes, parfaits, or just to serve over ice cream. In this case, mangoes make up a filling, thickened by Minute tapioca as it cooks down. The crisp topping is baked in the oven. Bake the topping in advance, time the cooking of the filling right and you can serve up a perfectly warmed dessert just as your guests are finishing dinner.

This recipe is perfect for a smaller 2-quart cooker as the fruit will cook way down in volume. If you use a larger oval cooker the filling will end up in a shallow layer, as it would in a baking pan.

7 cups diced ripe mango (about 4 pounds whole fruit)
2/3 cup unpacked brown sugar (more or less depending on sweetness of mango)
2 teaspoons lemon juice
1-1/2 tablespoons Minute tapioca

Topping:
1/2 cup flour
2 tablespoons white sugar
1/4 cup packed brown sugar
1/4 cup butter
1 teaspoon vanilla
1/2 teaspoon cinnamon
1/4 cup chopped macadamia nuts (may substitute almonds or pecans)

Combine mango, brown sugar, lemon juice, and tapioca in slow cooker. Cook on low 4 hours, or until fruit is very soft. If using a 2-quart cooker, stir once halfway through.

Meanwhile, make topping: Preheat oven to 350°F. Cut flour and sugars into butter. Add vanilla and cinnamon, mix in well. Stir in nuts. Spread evenly over a baking sheet in uniform clumps. Bake 15 to 20 minutes, stirring occasionally, until toasted and brown. (Topping can be baked a day or two ahead and stored in an airtight container.)

Remove mango filling to a serving dish and sprinkle with topping. If using an oval slow cooker, filling can be topped and served right out of the crock.

Chocolate Ensemada Bread Pudding Cake

Serves 8

An ensemada is a pastry with Spanish origins, best known in Hawai'i in its Filipino version—an oversized, soft bun slathered in butter and sugar. It has no nutritional value—in fact it has negative value. So how about we make it even worse by adding chocolate! and eggs! and more sugar!

Most slow cooker recipes for bread pudding call for setting up a water bath, as you would when baking in the oven, but I've found this yields very mushy results. This version instead emerges firm and cakelike. The ensemada brings its own butter and sugar, giving the dish a good head start.

4 to 5 ensemada buns broken in pieces to make 4-1/2 cups
1/4 cup bittersweet chocolate chips
1/2 cup chopped nuts, optional

Sauce:
1-1/2 cups coconut milk
1/2 cup bittersweet chocolate chips
1/2 cup sugar
2 teaspoons cinnamon
1 teaspoon vanilla
2 eggs

Spread ensemada pieces out in baking pan and let dry overnight, turning once.

Grease a 2-quart slow cooker (see note). Line with large

square of foil, letting foil extend above the rim to help remove cooked cake.

Place ensemada pieces in mixing bowl and toss with 1/4 cup chocolate chips and nuts, if using.

To make sauce: Heat coconut milk over medium heat (do not let boil). Add chocolate chips and sugar, stir to dissolve. Stir in cinnamon and vanilla.

Whisk eggs in separate bowl. Add a spoonful of the milk mixture, whisking to warm eggs. Slowly add remaining milk, whisking to combine so eggs do not curdle. Pour mixture over bread pieces and toss to coat. Spoon into crock. Cook on low 3 hours, until firm. A knife inserted into pudding should come out clean except for a possible smear of chocolate. Turn off heat, remove lid and let cool 30 minutes.

Use foil to lift bread pudding onto serving plate. It will be firm enough to slice in wedges like a cake.

{ NOTE } If you don't have a mini-cooker, this pudding can be cooked in a 2-quart baking dish that fits inside a 6- or 7-quart slow cooker. Or, double the recipe and cook it in a larger crock. Cooking time may be an hour longer.

Liliko'i Cheesecake

Cheesecakes "bake" up beautifully in a slow cooker, although you can't make the standard 10-inch size. You will need a round baking dish that fits in your slow cooker. A 1-1/2- or 2-quart casserole fits nicely in larger cookers, either oval or round, and produces a cute 8-inch cheesecake perfect for smaller parties. You'll be pouring boiling water into the cooker and lowering the casserole into the water, creating a water bath that will give your cheesecake its silky texture.

16 ounces cream cheese, softened
3/4 cup sugar
1 tablespoon flour
1/2 cup half-and-half
2 large eggs
1/4 cup liliko'i (passion fruit) purée
1 teaspoon vanilla

Crust:
3/4 cup graham cracker crumbs
1 tablespoon melted butter

Line a 2-quart baking dish with large square of foil, extending above rim; grease foil. Bring 2 cups water to boil.

Combine cracker crumbs with butter; press into bottom of baking dish.

Whip cream cheese until smooth. Beat in sugar and flour, then half-and-half and eggs until mixture is smooth. Stir in

liliko'i and vanilla. Pour into baking dish.

Pour boiling water into a 6- or 7-quart slow cooker. Slowly ease baking dish into cooker. Drape a clean towel over cooker so that condensation will not drip onto cheesecake. Place lid over towel. Cook on high 2 to 3 hours, until cheesecake is set. Turn off cooker and remove lid and towel. Let cheesecake sit in cooker as it cools to allow it to firm up. Top will collapse slightly. Chill well.

Unmold by grasping the edges of the foil and lifting the whole cake out of the baking dish and onto a serving dish.

{ VARIATIONS } Any type of fruit purée can be substituted for the liliko'i, or eliminate the purée and make a vanilla cheesecake (you may need to add a little more half-and-half to the batter to make it smooth enough).

Coconut Pudding with Tapioca Pearls

Makes 8 dessert cups

Tapioca pearls are tiny globules made from tapioca starch that balloon up once cooked to resemble fish eggs. A pudding made with pearls thickens without the use of flour or cornstarch, the pearls being a starch in themselves. It's easy—and a slow cooker makes it even easier by eliminating any danger of scorching. This dish is portioned for a small, 2-quart slow cooker.

1/2 cup small pearl tapioca (sold in Asian markets)
3 cups water
Pinch salt
1 (13-ounce) can coconut milk
1/2 cup sugar
1 teaspoon vanilla extract
1/4 cup guava or passion fruit juice
1 cup chopped fruit (mango, banana, strawberries, honeydew
    melon, kiwi or lychee are all good)

Place tapioca pearls and water in 2-quart slow cooker. Add salt. Cook on high until pearls turn from white to translucent, 2 to 3 hours. Don't be concerned if nothing seems to be happening for the first hour. The heat has to rise enough for the water to simmer.

Mixture will be thick and sticky; stir well, then add coconut milk and sugar. (If coconut milk has been chilled, warm in microwave before adding.) Stir until sugar dissolves. Add vanilla. Taste, adding more sugar if necessary. Divide among 8 dessert cups. Chill until firm.

Pour a thin layer of juice over each cup of pudding. Top with fruit.

{ VARIATION } Stir 1/4 cup fruit purée into pudding with vanilla. Strawberries, peaches, guava, or passion fruit are good options.

{ NOTE } This recipe yields a pudding that is quite firm once chilled, relaxing a little as it sits at room temperature. For a softer pudding, soak pearls in water 10 minutes, drain, then put pearls in slow cooker with fresh water. This will remove some of the starch.

Chocolate Mochi Cake

Serves 12

Chewier than a cake but not as fudgy as a brownie, a slice of mochi cake is "bouncy," says Beth An Nishijima of Nori's Saimin & Snacks in Hilo, who developed this beloved snack. The Nori's version is baked in loaf pans. This is basically a half-recipe with a couple of adjustments for the slow cooker.

2-1/4 cups mochiko
2-1/4 cups sugar
2-1/2 tablespoons unsweetened cocoa powder
1 teaspoon baking powder
1 (13-ounce) can coconut milk
2 eggs, beaten
1/2 tablespoon vanilla extract
1/4 cup butter, melted

Line a 1-1/2- or 2-quart round ceramic baking dish with large square of foil, allowing foil to extend above the rim of the dish (cake will rise all the way to the rim).

Combine mochiko, sugar, cocoa powder, and baking powder. Whisk to combine evenly. In a separate bowl combine coconut milk, eggs, vanilla extract, and butter. Add to dry mixture and stir until batter is smooth. Pour batter into baking dish and place dish in a 6- or 7-quart slow cooker. Cook on high 3 hours, until set in center. Remove lid and let cake set as the cooker cools.

Remove dish from cooker. When cake is cooled, remove from dish by lifting the foil. Peel off foil and cut cake into pieces with plastic knife.